Contents

The dentist's surgery

A dentist's surgery is where people go to have their teeth checked and looked after.

There is a **reception** desk and a waiting area where **patients** wait to see their dentist.

Each dentist has a room full of **equipment** and **instruments** to check and treat a patient's teeth.

The patient's chair can be moved up or down, and tipped backwards so the dentist can see easily into a patient's mouth.

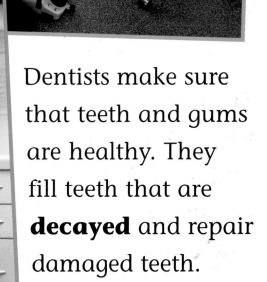

Dentists make sure that teeth and gums are healthy. They fill teeth that are **decayed** and repair damaged teeth.

The team

Here are some of the surgery team. As well as dentists, there are dental nurses, **receptionists** and a **manager**.

Sandra is a dental nurse. She helps the dentist by sorting instruments and looking after patients.

Selina is the manager. This means she is in charge of the day-to-day running of the surgery.

Kelly is a receptionist. She works at the reception desk, answering phone calls, greeting patients and sorting out **appointments**.

James is one of the four dentists working in the surgery.

Starting work

Jill is a dentist and the owner of the surgery. She opens up the surgery each morning.

Selina, the manager, turns on her computer and looks at the appointment list for the day.

Saba is a dentist too. She looks at the diary on her computer to see when her first patient is coming in. Then she checks the **patient notes**.

Dental nurse Louise finds all the notes that Saba needs for her patients today.

'The patient notes are very important. They hold all the information a dentist needs to treat a patient well.'
Saba, dentist

At the reception

Kelly greets all the patients when they arrive. She also helps them fill in **forms**, and takes payment for **treatments**.

Mike is a new patient, so Kelly helps him fill in a form.

'I like chatting with patients and putting them at ease.'
Kelly, receptionist

Mike reads a magazine while he waits for his appointment.

In reception there are things that patients can buy to help them look after their teeth.

Deliveries

Some patients need **false teeth**, or parts such as **crowns** to repair damaged teeth. These parts are made in a **laboratory**. Boxes of false teeth and other parts are delivered to the surgery every day.

Having a check-up

Amy is having a check-up. While Sandra gets Amy ready, Jill chats to her about her last visit to the surgery.

'It's important to talk to patients and explain what you're going to do.'
Jill, dentist

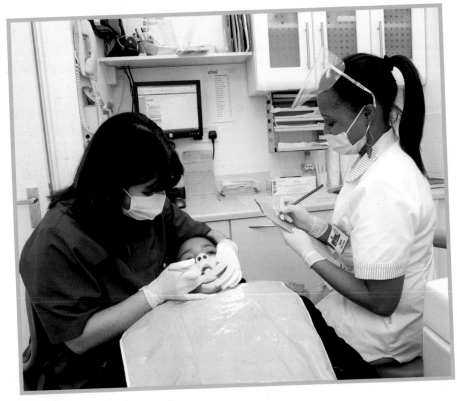

Jill checks Amy's teeth and Sandra makes notes. Sandra writes down any changes to Amy's teeth.

After the check-up, Jill talks to Amy about brushing her teeth.

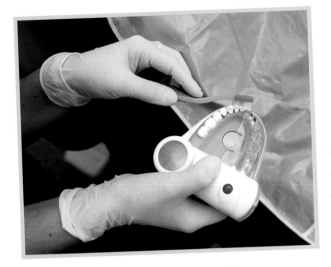

Jill has a model of some teeth to show Amy the best way to brush.

Foods for healthy teeth and gums

Brushing your teeth is important, but eating plenty of fresh fruit and vegetables will help to keep your teeth and gums healthy. Sweets, biscuits and fizzy drinks contain lots of sugar which is bad for your teeth, and they do not provide your body with the goodness you need to keep healthy.

Having a filling

Jill says goodbye to Amy. Then she calls in her next patient, Mike.

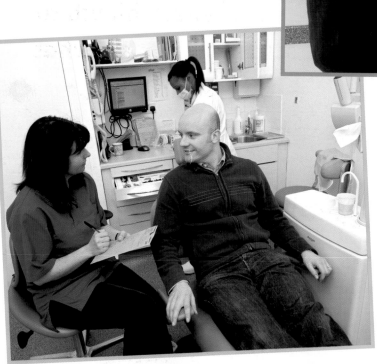

As Mike is a new patient, Jill chats with him about any problems he has with his teeth.

Jill checks all Mike's teeth carefully and decides that Mike needs one filling. She also takes an **x-ray** (see page 16).

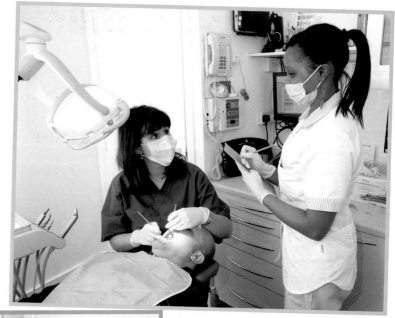

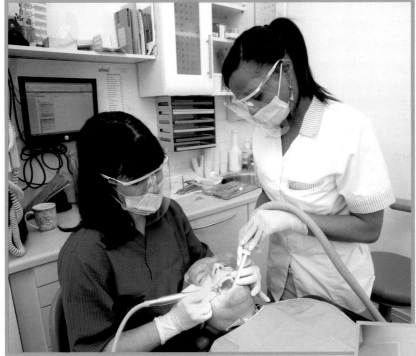

Jill drills and fills Mike's tooth. Sandra shines a bright light into Mike's mouth so Jill can see what she is doing.

Mike rinses his mouth when the filling is finished.

Taking an x-ray

Dentists sometimes take an x-ray to help them see how best to treat a tooth.

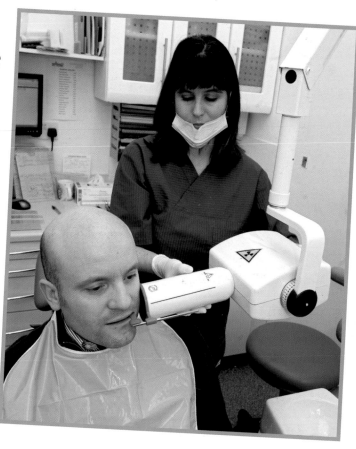

Jill lines up the x-ray machine. The machine is fixed on the wall on a long metal arm so it is easy to put in the right position.

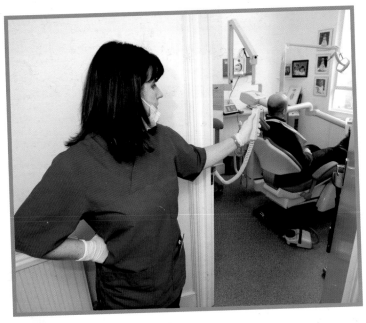

Jill stays outside the room as the x-ray is taken. There is no danger for patients, but the **radiation** might be a problem if Jill stayed in the room every time an x-ray was taken.

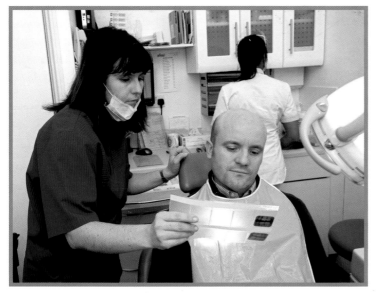

Jill looks at the x-ray picture with the patient. The x-ray shows what is wrong and helps Jill decide what treatment is needed.

Developing an x-ray

Once an x-ray has been taken it needs to be **developed** before a dentist can see the picture.

Dental nurse Lesley operates the x-ray developing machine.

Film is fed through the machine. A few minutes later the picture is clear.

The surgery manager

The surgery manager, Selina, makes sure the dentists and nurses have all the equipment and **supplies** they need. She makes phone calls to find out when deliveries of supplies will arrive.

In the storeroom, Selina unpacks a box of supplies. She makes sure everything is put away carefully so that everyone can find what they need.

Saba has booked a holiday, so Selina talks about who will cover her work while she is away.

Selina makes sure all the patient notes are filed away carefully.

Selina has a visit from Sue. Sue works for a company that sells dental supplies. Selina orders some new supplies.

Emergency treatment

Sorcha has come in for **emergency** treatment. She fell over in the playground and knocked her front teeth.

As soon as Sorcha arrives she goes into Saba's surgery. Saba looks at Sorcha's teeth to check if they are broken or loose.

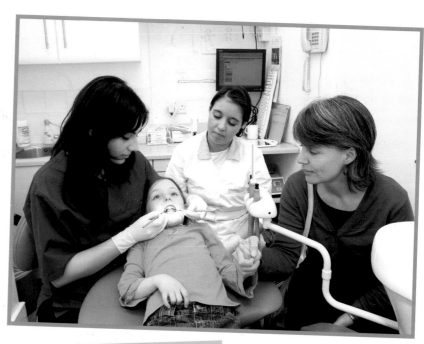

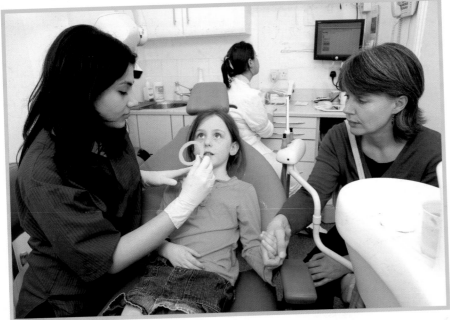

Saba is going to take some x-rays to check Sorcha's teeth.

Saba checks the x-rays and decides the teeth are not damaged.

Saba says Sorcha's teeth will be fine.

Knocked teeth

Sometimes teeth are knocked during games and sports. You can hold a wet tissue over your mouth to help stop the pain.

If a tooth is knocked out, try to push it gently back into the socket. Or put the tooth in milk or **saliva** to keep it wet. Go straight to your dentist or to a hospital.

Brushing teeth

James has checked Thomas's teeth, and he thinks Thomas is not brushing his teeth well. Thomas chews a tablet that colours his teeth red. This shows any **plaque** on the teeth.

James holds up a mirror so Thomas can see his teeth.

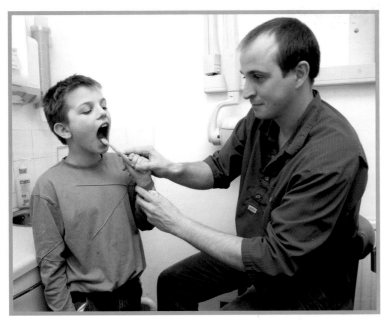

The red colouring shows Thomas where he needs to brush his teeth more carefully.

'Children need to get into the habit of taking good care of their teeth.'

James, dentist

Toothcare tips

Choose a toothbrush that feels right for you, and remember to get a new toothbrush regularly. Brush your teeth for two minutes twice a day, using a blob of

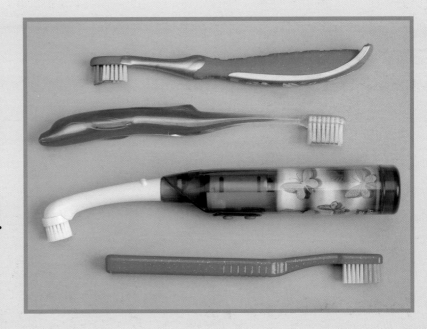

toothpaste the size of a pea. Use gentle brush strokes, and always brush the back teeth too. Spit out the toothpaste when you have finished.

A dental nurse's job

The dental nurses clean and sort the instruments after each patient leaves, and then get the room ready for the next patient.

Louise carries in a tray of clean instruments for the dentist to use.

'I make sure all the instruments are cleaned and sorted, ready to be used.'
Louise, dental nurse

While Jill puts on her mask and gloves to do a check-up, Sandra makes sure she has all the right equipment ready.

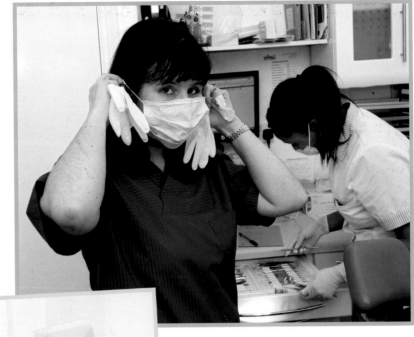

Lesley checks an x-ray to make sure it has developed properly.

Dental nurses also mix up pastes and filling mixtures for the dentist.

Health and safety

Dentists and nurses wear a mask over their mouth and nose when treating patients. This is to avoid spreading or catching **germs**.

'Making sure we don't spread or catch germs is very important in our work.'
Jill, dentist

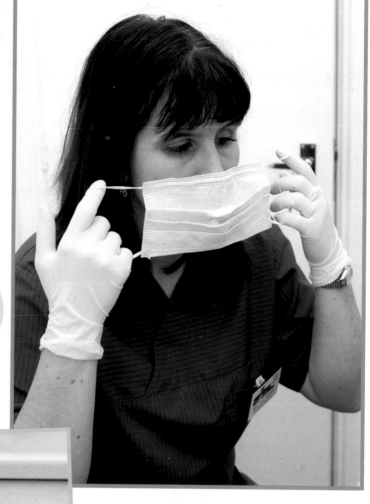

Dentists spend most of their time close to patients' mouths, touching their teeth and gums. Dentists use a new pair of **latex** gloves to check each patient.

Keeping instruments clean

The instruments that are used to work on teeth and gums are **sterilised** after every use. Dental nurse Vicki puts the instruments into a sterilising machine.

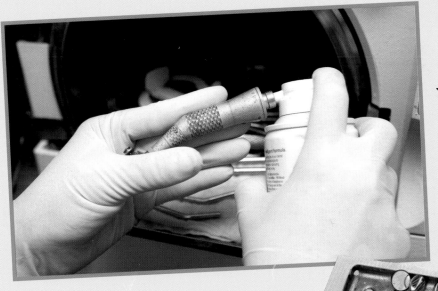

Vicki sprays the drills with oil.

Once the instruments are sterilised, Vicki puts them away ready to be used again.

Finishing work

It is the end of a busy day, and the last patients leave the surgery.

Dental nurse Vicki clears up after her last patient. She washes the instruments so they are ready to be sterilised.

The surgery team finish their work for the day.

Manager Selina makes a note of medical supplies she needs to order in the morning.

Once everybody has left the building, Jill locks the doors and rolls down the shutters.

 Glossary

appointments times booked to do something.

crowns the visible part of a tooth. If it is broken or decayed a new one is made and fitted.

decayed rotten material.

developed treated with chemicals to make a picture.

emergency something that needs urgent action.

equipment things you need to do a task.

false teeth a new set of teeth made to fit in the mouth over the gums.

forms pieces of paper to write down information.

germs tiny living things that can cause illness or infection.

instruments tools used by a dentist or surgeon.

laboratory a place with special equipment to make medical parts.

latex a thin stretchy material.

manager someone who is in charge of a place of work.

patient notes a folder of information about a patient and their dental health.

patients people who are being treated by a dentist or doctor.

plaque a sticky substance on a tooth that can cause decay.

radiation rays that make an x-ray picture that show bones and other parts inside the body.

reception a place in a building to welcome visitors.

receptionists people who work in a reception.

saliva a clear liquid made in the mouth.

sterilised to use steam and chemicals to make something clean and kill germs.

supplies things to be used.

treatments medicines or surgery to make a patient better.

x-ray a picture that shows bones and other parts inside the body.

Further information

Websites

www.kindandental.com Visit this website to find out more about the dentist's surgery featured in this book.

www.dentalhealth.org.uk The British Health Foundation website, with good links and advice on looking after your teeth.

www.ada.org The American Dental Association. Lots of advice and information and a good mix of games and puzzles.

Books

Dentist (When I'm At Work series), Deborah Chancellor, Franklin Watts, 2005

Your Teeth (Look After Yourself series), Claire Llewellyn, Franklin Watts, 2004

Every effort has been made by the Packagers and Publishers to ensure that these websites contain no inappropriate or offensive material. However, because of the nature of the Internet, it is impossible to guarantee that the contents of these sites will not be altered. We strongly advise that Internet access is supervised by a responsible adult.

Index